ISBN 979-8-9985846-0-2

Published by One World Media

Practical Happiness

The Technology of Creating Joy

Practical Happiness

The Technology of Creating Joy

Dale Kershner

Contents

Contents

If at first you
don't Succeed...

Try doing
what your

COACH

told you to do
the first time.

I am an Executive Coach.

My life has been dedicated to working with people in order to have them accomplish amazing things and have amazing experiences. As I sit here writing this book, I have been coaching for over 39 years.

In my nearly half century of coaching, I have helped people gain vast quantities of money, cars, boats, businesses, homes, jobs, promotions, relationships, children that behave and flourish and just about every conceivable thing one could ask for.

As a Coach for human beings, I am constantly seeking new and more efficient methods to bring my clients to their desired outcomes.

It is the rare soul that wishes to accumulate money for the sake of having more money. Generally, people want more money for the security it provides or for the cooler stuff they can buy. Sometimes accumulating money is simply to mark the score of the game;

"S/he who dies with the most money, wins".

I started to ask people what prompted them to want the stuff they were asking for.

Of course, the answers were very diverse. Most of the conversations were very similar in the final analysis.

"If I have boat loads of cash, I won't have to worry anymore."

"A shiny new sports car will cause girls/boys men/women to want to be with me."

"A big house will show my friends that I am successful."

But regardless of what they told me, what it came down to, and this should come as no surprise, the money/cars/homes/etc. Simply made people happier.

It was all about being happy, or being happier.

I realized that I had been taking all of my clients down a very long road to reach a simple destination.

It takes diligent focus and hard work to make piles of money.

It takes a lot of practice to change behavior patterns in people.

Repetition is the only way to move people into the patterns that serve the goals they have.

So why not show them how to be happy, no matter what?

Happy people are more successful, have better friendships/ relationships/marriages. Happy people tend to draw other happy people in to their circle of acquaintances. Perhaps the most direct way to provide people what they really want, is to show them how to be happy.

When you are happy, it is easier to make more money.

When you are happy, it is easier to find better relationships.

When you are happy, you can get the job of your dreams.

We humans generally have it backwards.

People mostly think that they need to have things to make them happy. Money, cars, boats, houses, etc.

Work hard...

Make money...

Buy things...

Be happy...

However this is the opposite of the best avenue to happiness.

Be happy FIRST, and all of the THINGS that you desire will either flow to you, or stop being important to you.

BE HAPPY

Make money

Buy stuff (if you wish)

Choose to be happy when YOU want to be happy. Stop relying on your circumstances or things around to to dictate your feelings or your experiences of life. Be happy in every situation. Be happy when you choose to be happy. Be happy in spite of the way the World occurs.

Be Happy.

I offer this book for your consideration.

This book contains my collected wisdom, my processes, tools and energy structures that I have learned over the years, about what it takes to be happy and have a happy life.

No matter what.

As you read this book you may recognize concepts from spirituality, Buddhism, neuroplasticity, quantum physics, Behaviorism, common sense and many other disciplines. I have drawn from every experience and source I have encountered to create this collected work. I have used every tool and technique extensively on myself before I let any client use them or before I included them in this book.

My life has been the classroom and testing
ground for all of these methods.

I have launched dozens of businesses. Some have succeeded wonderfully, and some have failed miserably. I have been taken advantage of. I have had hundreds of thousands stolen from me. I have been stiffed by clients for more than half a million dollars. I have been conned, married and divorced, had three heart attacks, died twice, lost the love of my life to cancer. All of the occurrences of this existence I have encountered, have been so that I could learn how to create happiness in every and any situation.

Through every trial, through every hardship, I learned how to be happy when I chose to. I learned to overcome my circumstances and choose in every moment how I wanted to be. I bring 68 years of life to this work.

Now, I can pass all of this on to you.

PRACTICAL HAPPINESS

The Technology of Creating Joy

Chapter

How to be Happy no Matter What

You are the author of your emotions.

You choose how to feel in any given situation.

Again:

YOU ARE THE AUTHOR OF YOUR EMOTIONS!

No matter what is going on…

CHOOSE TO BE HAPPY.

It is that simple. Believe it or not, it is truly that simple.

If that did it for you, AWESOME! Please pass this book on
to a friend and spend the rest of your life being happy.

I said it was simple, but I didn't say it was easy. Perhaps it would be useful to have some strategy and support.

Welcome to the rest of this book...

Don't wait until
you are rich
to be happy.

Happiness
is FREE!

Chapter

Why Aren't we Happy All of the Time?

You choose your emotions.

"My daughter makes me so angry."

"My Boss is so completely frustrating."

"This movie makes me so sad."

"I am depressed because I don't have any friends."

All of these are lies. I don't mean that for you the movie is not sad, or that your boss has behaviors that set you off. I mean that your emotions do not happen as a result of external circumstance.

You make them all up.

You may already be aware of this.

Quiet your thoughts and give up your right to be right for a moment. (more about this later) Open your mind and allow all possibilities to flow.

When something happens in your life, you take the thing that happened and add to it an emotion or feeling. The circumstance does not actually mean what you say it means. Plus, your meaning is personal to just you. This is a multi-step process for humans, but seems instantaneous. The thing happens, you attach a meaning to the thing that happened and then you create an emotional reaction to the meaning you created about the thing that happened.

Think about it this way: When you were young, you were riding in the car with your mom. You got the idea that an ice cream cone would be the perfect treat at that precise moment.

"Mom, I want an ice cream cone." You say. Mom responds, "No, you can't have an ice cream right now because we are about to have lunch and you will spoil your appetite."

Instantly you have a response.

You may pout, cry, scream, kick her seat, etc. But something fires off inside you to illicit a response.

Now notice that there is an entire spectrum of possible responses from which you can choose. You chose whatever you chose in that moment. You could choose relief, depression, joy or gratitude, anger, loss.

Regardless, your young mind creates some emotional response to Mom saying "no."

Other children would, and do choose alternate feelings for the same circumstance. Just like adults choose all sorts of responses to the same situations.

The important part is that you choose.

In that singular moment you may have experienced no for the first time. Perhaps this is the first time you were ever denied something that you wanted. Imagine the shock to your toddler mind that for the first time in your life, the answer is "no".

You have lived your life since that moment gathering evidence that your chosen response to your mother's stinginess or similar experience is the "correct" response.

You have practiced this over and over again. You have come to similar conclusions thousands and even tens of, or hundreds of thousands of times. As a matter of fact, you have practiced this response so many times, that you have perfected it. You no longer need to think about it. It happens automatically. As a matter of fact, it is now your "true" response.

You may have even created this response as "THE TRUTH".

Take a moment to reflect back over some meanings you have created in this last week.

Now let's take an action to underline this concept.

Action:

Take out a piece of paper and something to write with.

Think about a recent emotional experience. Something that you reacted to with anger, fear, sadness or some other strong emotion.

Did you find one?

Write a short description of what happened to make you feel this way.

Under the description, write the emotion that you felt in that moment. Now, under that emotion draw a line.

_____

Then, under the line, write a different emotion than the one you had in the particular situation. i.e. If it made you mad, write down sad.

Now write down four other possible emotions that could have happened as a result of the thing that happened. They don't have to be emotions you experienced, just different emotions. They do not even need to relate to this situation. They just need to be an emotion.

Stop for a moment and read the list of emotions.

Draw another line.

_____

Under that line, write five humorous emotions that could have happened as a result of the situation.

Draw another line.

_____

Under that line, write five dangerous emotions that could happen as a result of the situation.

Draw another line.

_____

Under that line write five happy emotions that could happen as a result of the situation.

Pick up this book again and start reading.

This exercise is designed to have you see that there are an unlimited number of possible reactions to any given situation. You just have created your favorite set of them.

If you are not yet able to see the point of the exercise, go back to your sheet of paper and draw another line and then list the following:

_____

Significant emotions for your situation

_____

Mean emotions

_____

Religious emotions

_____

Angry emotions

_____

Enlightened emotions

_____

Smart emotions

By now you should be getting the point.

In your past, you have practiced your emotional responses so much that you have even mapped your responses into the way your brain fires. You created neuro pathways consistent with your responses. You actually altered the physical structure in your brain by thinking and reacting the same way over and over again. We call this "creating brain patterns" or "mapping neuro pathways".

You may be sitting there and thinking "if these patterns are physically in my brain, how am I supposed to change my patterns?"

I am glad you asked.

YOU created the patterns in the first place. AND you did so without knowing you were doing this. So, now that you know you did this, you can create new patterns, new ways for your brain to fire, by INTENTIONALLY creating new habits or patterns.

There are three stages to creating new neuro pathways:

NIC (Notice, Interrupt, Change) Tool:

1.   Notice your current emotion or reaction to the circumstance.

This may sound simple, (because it is) but may not be as easy in practice.

You have worked for so many years developing your reactions, that they are now automatic. Like I mentioned before, your emotions seem like the "true" emotion to have in that moment.

2.   Interrupt the emotion/reaction.

The point here is to stop the action after you have noticed the reaction to the given circumstance or happening.

3.   Create a new, more workable reaction.

Once you have noticed and then interrupted the emotion or reaction that is not working for you, now you can insert one that does.

Let's discuss right and wrong, good and bad.

To start with, the concepts of right and wrong, good and bad are mythology. As humans, we have bought into a rating system designed by humans and then passed on to other humans. Society has taken it upon itself to vote that the majority vote by people is evidence of the truth.

Right and wrong, good and bad are opinions that
differ with every human. And in every situation.

Notice that we have laws that dictate these values for us. These laws are created and ratified by the majority of the citizens. This then creates a type of "workability". But even these rights and wrongs are adjudicated before consequences are applied.

For the purposes of our discussion, you may assume that there are no universal, rights, nor wrongs. No good, nor bad.

What we are striving for is workability.

A life that works, and by our own individual assessment.

Ok, back to our new pattern...

Here is how we accomplish step one, or noticing the pattern we wish to replace.

Please look back over this past week. In doing so, you could most likely pick out a handful of times that you reacted to a situation in a manner that in retrospect, you may have chosen an alternate reaction or emotion.

Are you thinking of one?

Ok, for the next two weeks, carry a small note pad and pen or pencil and make a tic mark on your pad every time you notice that you experience the emotion. One mark for each time this situation comes up again and you experience this undesired response.

That's it. You are now training yourself to notice every time that emotion shows up. You will also notice that you are much more aware of other emotions and reactions you have in different situations. But let's just focus on this first one for the next two weeks. Now you may find that this step takes less or more than two weeks. Take the time you need to so that you readily see the emotion show up every time.

> You may not notice until the end of your day.

That is fine. Still make your tic mark. Then as you practice, you will get to the point where you notice the pattern more and more quickly.

You may want to put sticky notes up to remind you to be on the look-out for the emotion. Makes sure to change the color, position or wording on the notes after seven days.

> Any reminder will disappear after seven
> days of unchanged positioning.

Step two:

> We are going to interrupt the emotion or
> pattern that you wish to change.

The most effective way to do this is to use a body movement. The body registers in the brain several seconds more rapidly than emotions or intellectual thought. This is why we engage the body in our pattern training.

Here is how: Take the first two fingers of your right hand and lay them across the wrist of your left arm like you are taking your pulse. (you need not actually take your pulse) Simply make contact with your left wrist.

This contact initiates the interruption. You can remove your fingers after a second. The idea is to simply make the body contact.

Note: any contact will suffice. Create what works best for you. I have provided this technique as an easy and inconspicuous movement.

The next thing to do is to take three deep cleansing breaths. In through the nose, out through the nose. These breaths should be very slow and as deep as you can make them. When you have inhaled all of the air you can, take in just a bit more. When you have exhaled completely, let out just a bit more air.

> Make sure to focus all of your attention on your breathing.
> This is a mindfulness practice to empty your mind of
> the pattern or behavior you are seeking to modify.

After three deep breaths, whatever unwanted emotion that was about to take you over, is dissipated to the degree that you can control and even replace it.

You have already done your tic mark work, haven't you?

Having done so, you will now readily notice when an emotion is about to show up that you wish to replace. This is how to interrupt these emotions every time. Don't get frustrated if you are not able to notice and interrupt these occurrences the first time. This will come with practice.

Remember that you have practiced for years, probably decades your old emotional responses to your circumstances. Now that you are conscious to this, it will take much less time to reprogram yourself to establish new replacement emotions.

That leads us to our final step in this process.

Create a new emotion or reaction for this circumstance.

You now notice your behavior and the reaction you have to the circumstance, you also know how to interrupt the previous emotion or reaction. Now choose your desired response (more workable response) and actively choose your created response at the completion of your three breaths.

Perhaps you wish to experience more peace and tranquility in your life. So, now, whenever you notice anger or anxiety, interrupt it and create peace.

Or maybe you simply want to be happy. The next time (and every time) you notice yourself being upset or depressed. Interrupt that emotion and create happy.

You may be thinking that all of this is an over simplification. That it cannot be this simple. Well, consider that you got yourself here by doing these things exactly. You practiced your responses to the circumstances around you over and over until they became the truth for you. You got so good at the response, you no longer even have to think about it, it is automatic.

You created and practiced your TRUTH

Do the same thing now. Only this time consciously choose your response to situations. And then practice. Keep practicing until the new response becomes second nature and you don't even have to think about it anymore. This will take a while. You may have to create reminder and existence systems in order to keep yourself practicing your new emotions and responses.

Someone cuts you off in traffic, smile. Someone yells at you, be peaceful.

Insert your own behavior here...

This is not the same as bottling up your emotions or suppressing them. The point here is to acknowledge your feelings and emotions. Sometimes you may find it useful to intensely express them. I.e. Set aside five minutes to throw a tantrum. (Please be responsible for where and when you do this.)

Over time, the tantrums serve you less and less in that you realize that they are your creation and you can create whatever you wish. Soon you may discover that you need take shorter periods of time for your emotional release practice to the point where the release happens almost instantaneously.

Be patient. You have taken YEARS to develop your emotional reactions. It may take years to create a new way of being. I promise, it won't take as long as it took to become who you are right now, as you will be aware of these new creations.

Train

your mind

to see the

good in

everything

Chapter

Neuroplasticity

Neuroplasticity refers to the lifelong capacity of the human brain to change and rewire how it fires in response to the stimulation of learning, experience and repetition.

Long story short, you can at any point in your life, change the way you respond to situations or even modify lifelong behaviors. This is the point of the exercise in the prior chapter. You can identify and then modify your reactions and behaviors through repetitive conscious substitution.

Your brain is elastic, mold-able. You are not stuck with anything you wish to change. Anything. You got here by unconsciously practicing and reinforcing your emotions and behaviors. You can get where you want to go through the practice of new and repeated emotions and behaviors.

This is why I constructed the exercise in the previous chapter the way I did.

In the exercise, we use physical interruption and repetition to reprogram the way your brain fires. The difference between how you programmed your brain in the first place and how we are doing it now, is you are fully conscious to the process. I believe that this is why we can remap your brain processes much more rapidly than you did initially.

Repetition was what created your synapse pathways in the first place, repetition is how to create new pathways now.

We have all heard the old adage that "you can't teach an old dog new tricks". Understanding neuroplasticity, we can see that it may take more practice to learn new tricks, but it is far from impossible to learn new tricks, or ways of being. We human beings are constantly evolving and changing our reactions and behaviors.

We may choose to remain a victim of our habits and trapped in our behaviors, but all of that is up to you. Once you decide to make the change you want to make, it is as simple as practicing the new behavior over and over again until it becomes the new habit.

The new way your brain fires.

The more you practice the new you, the more rapidly you become the new you. Even if you feel like the new emotions are inauthentic, go ahead and pretend that you are experiencing them. The concept of "fake it until you make it" is very valid here. Even if you feel silly doing the things I have described up until here in this book, keep doing them until they stop feeling silly and ultimately become your new behaviors.

Unprotected empathy

is self destruction

Chapter

Protect Your Energy

Are you an Empath?

Regardless of your answer, it is my belief that everyone has empathic sensitivities at some level. Some of us feel everyone's emotions and even feelings as if they were our own. Some people walk around seemingly oblivious to everything and everyone around them. Regardless of where you find yourself on this scale of empathy, you are constantly being impacted by the energies around you.

This section is about how to protect yourself as you move around the World among other people. Often, we are unaware that much of the burden and baggage we carry, came from those around us, or even from the World at large.

Have you ever been shopping during the holidays and once you got home you feel completely exhausted even though you really did not experience that much physical exertion?

Have you ever walked into a room and it felt heavy or sad even before you spoke or observed anyone?

Have you ever had the experience of being watched even though you could see no one?
These are all examples of empathic feelings.

For the scientist, all humans emit some form of energy. It may be electro-magnetic, it may be heat or could be emissions at the quantum level. Regardless of the form of energy, one would have to agree that this energy is measurable to some degree if we are close to the human (emitter). As we move away from the source we would expect that the measurable emission would get smaller and smaller depending upon the sensitivity of our measuring device. Certainly, current science has limits as to be able to test this energy. An EMF (Electro-magnetic Field) device can only sense electro-magnetic energy out to six feet or so. Yet if we could devise a more sensitive tool, we might discover that humans emit energy in extremely wide circles. Maybe even thousands of miles?

It, then, is no surprise if we feel impacted when many people are affected in a negative manner. (9/11, school shootings, riots etc.)

If this section of the book occurs as complete hogwash, you may skip to the next chapter. If, however, there seems to be a glimmer of possibility in my description, you may wish to read on.

You are aware that energy, in various forms, is all around us.

From the day of our birth, we are bombarded by all sorts of energy and this leaves an indelible impression. We may have grown up around love and kindness which is a form of energetic field. We may have grown up around fear and anger which is another form of energy field.

Rarely are we taught how to manage the energy we pass through as we journey on the pathway of our lives. It is impossible not to be impacted by the energies out in society at large. Mass shootings of school children, bombings, clock tower snipers, mid-east unrest, wars, pandemics, the list goes on and on. Simply watching the evening news exposes us to a constant stream of negative energy.

Perhaps you have noticed that your mood sours after watching the news. Perhaps this happens after a night out on the town? Regardless, you have noticed in your past that your emotions are impacted by forces outside yourself on a regular basis.

This is the life of an empath.

A full-blown empath has these experiences, but amplified tremendously. My point is that we all have this experience on some level. I am offering this section to provide tools to avoid these impacts and to do something about them after it has happened. After your person has accumulated negative energy either short term or long.

Long term exposure and accumulation can lead to emotional changes, but also can manifest in illness such as heart disease and cancer.

I think all disease has some basis in accumulated negative energy.

What follows is a simple method to keep yourself from absorbing the energies out there that influence how you feel and the blockages to your own happiness. The most obvious solution to negative energy exposure is to not expose yourself to negative energy. Avoid the news. You can stay informed without hearing all of the horrible things that happened in the World today.

Action:

There are four basic elements. Air, Water, Earth and Fire. You will find that you have an affinity toward one of these elements over the other three.

For many empaths, the element that works the best for grounding and protection is Water.

For this exercise, choose one of the elements that feels most comfortable. (you can always try other elements later)

I will use the element of Water for the example for this exercise.

This is a visualization tool. You will create a visualization to protect yourself from external energies.

Close your eyes.

You may open your eyes to read the instructions and then close them to do the exercise. Visualize a peaceful place. Someplace you are happy and calm.

Now "see" yourself suspended in the air above a body of water. You only need be a foot or two above the water source.

Now, in your visualization, draw the water up from the source to the bottom of your feet but not touching. Flare the water source out at this point to create a round platform beneath your feet.

Next, draw the water up from the edges of the platform to form walls of water in a cylinder surrounding you.

Now, above your head, draw the water back together to create a roof to your cylinder.

Next allow the water to complete a stream that flows up as far as you can see.

Make sure that water cylinder is flowing constantly. It should be from top to bottom, for our purposes.

Now imagine the energy on the outside of the cylinder hitting the wall of water and being stopped and carried down by the flow of the water. Continue to visualize this until you feel comfortable, calm and protected.

Now go out into the World feeling protected from the external influences of those outside your water cylinder.

If you wish, make this part of your morning ritual. It only takes a minute. As you practice this you will become more and more proficient in this creation. You may also find it useful to invoke this visualization at certain times during your day.

Before going to talk to your boss.

Before entering a room with large crowds of people.

Before a conversation with someone who is negative.

You may find it useful to invoke this protection visualization before walking into an important business meeting or a job interview. It never hurts to have more protection.

Second Energy Tool

This second tool is provided to get negative energy out of your body after a particularly challenging day or after taking on someone else's energy. I do this after providing energy healing.

Find a source of cool running water. A kitchen or bathroom faucet works well for this as does a stream in the woods.

Start the water flowing (the stream is already moving).

Now set the intention in your mind to allow the negative energy in your body to flow out of your hands.

Put your hands under the water and rub them together like you are washing them. Soap is optional.

While your hands are in the running water, intend the energy out of you and allow it to return to the Earth through the water.

Continue this until you feel that the negative energy is completely out of you and completely in the water.

Turn off the spigot.

There you go. You now have the two most important tools that an Empath uses to remain clear of unintended energy.

You may discover that different elements work better for you than water. Experiment with Earth (go oustsoide and stand barefoot on the ground and intend the energy into the soil), Fire (stand in the morning Sun and let your energy go in the warm beams of sunlight, or light a candle and give your negative energy to the flame), Air (stand in the breeze and let go of you energy into the wind).

You will find one of these practices to be most meaningfull to you. Go with or develop a practices that serves you the best.

You may find it useful to start your day with the protection routine if you are going to be out among people. You may also wish to use the energy cleanse process (hands under running water) when you come home to your sanctuary. You should also use this tool any time you have been exposed to stressful or difficult people. The sooner you can excuse yourself to a bathroom and let the unwanted energy flow out of you, the better.

Up to this point in this book, I have been discussing methods and tools to create and maintain happiness.

In any situation or in any place, you have the skill and the ability to invent happiness as your way of being.

The following chapters are designed to illustrate habits and behaviors that are making it more difficult to remain happy. Behaviors that steal away your happiness or surround you with pressures and pulls that make it harder to create and enjoy a happy life.

Why not reduce or eliminate the things we do in our lives that keep happiness away?

Why not indeed?

Patience is the calm
acceptance that things
can happen in a different
order then the one
you have in mind.

Chapter

Patience

Let's talk about patience. As you can see from the prior chapters, patience with yourself will be an important component of successful behavior change. Some of the skills I taught myself took years to become my default habits.

Patience, or the lack thereof, is a core experience for all of us that permeates all of our reactions and resultant emotions.

"That ticket clerk is lucky I don't lose my patience with the way this airline is treating me."

"If I wasn't so patient, I would have rammed my bumper into that driver who just cut me off."

"I'm losing my patience with all of the antics my kids are pulling today"

The common thread in the prior statements (other than that they are about patience) is that the speaker in each case is placing the need or cause for patience on an external circumstance.

In reality, patience, or the lack thereof is the creation of the speaker.

Your creation.

So is the need for it and the threshold at which it is required.

All of the aspects of patience, like every emotion and reaction for humans, are simply the result of years of practice and application leading to a set of standards under which we employ various levels of patience or lack thereof. After sufficient practice we become unconscious to our creations and instead see them as reality.

They become our truths.

It is no longer: Something happens (or doesn't happen) and then we have a reaction, but rather that the thing that happens is the source of our patience or impatience. It is a result of the circumstances and not our creation. Think about the last time you "lost your patience" and then think about what happened that caused you to loose your patience.

The "thing that happened" had nothing to do with you loosing you patience. You created and then practiced, for years, this reaction to similar things that have happened. You practiced so often that the circumstance has become the cause of your impatience.

Lack of patience makes us unhappy.

An abundance of patience makes us happy.

You can either sit there fuming about the plane delay, or you can be grateful for some additional time to meditate and people watch.

You can get angry with your children, or you can welcome the opportunity to learn something about engaging the kids and becoming involved with them at a new level.

Neither choice is the correct one, nor the incorrect one. We are talking, here, about how to achieve happiness.

How to create happiness as often as we can.

Whichever outcome seems the happiest choice to you, choose that one. But make sure to pay attention to the fact that you are choosing, that you are in the driver's seat.

Being more patient contributes to experiencing more happiness. When we learn to move in the World without the various situations dictating our reactions, we can create joy and happiness whenever we choose.

Action:

For the next seven days, (or forever) pay attention to the times you experience patience or impatience. Stop for a moment (if circumstances allow) and examine what is happening. What are the circumstances that lead you to the experience you are having.

Think back to similar situations where you have experienced similar levels of patience. Consider the connective thread. What is the same about those circumstances and the current situation? Think back to all (many) of the times when this occurred.

Ok, now, invent a new reaction to the current situation. If you are lacking patience, make up a reason why the scenario is a gift or positive outcome. If you are noticing that you have an abundance of patience, seek the reason why. Take that information and see where you can apply it in other situations that may be more challenging.

By spending time in this contemplation, you will give yourself access to noticing these situations in the future.

Step one, notice.

Now that you are seeing the circumstances as separate from the situation. This allows you to interrupt your automatic reaction.

Once you have interrupted your automatic response, you can create a different experience in these times of impatience.

Continue to practice these new creations. The more you practice this process, the more peaceful reactions will become natural for you.

Implement the tool from the second chapter. This is a great place to use the "Notice, Interrupt and Create" (NIC) technology.

The best time to plant a tree

was twenty years ago.

The second best time is now.

Latin Proverb

Chapter

Use Your Words

We have discussed some of the behaviors and habits that keep us from accomplishing a happy life. Now let's turn our focus to something we do every day and night. Something that can help us set the stage for our evolution to Happiness. Let's talk about how we speak.

The words we use.

This is the most direct and impactful area to make changes in our experience of the World and ourselves within it.

You have heard someone (or several people) say things like:

> "I have left several messages but they
> just don't want to call me back."

Or

> "I guess it's over since he hasn't texted me in three days."

This is a subtle point. The first example is a non-factual sentence. A conclusion is being drawn. Cause/effect. Non-response after numerous messages means an intent not to communicate.

A more factual way to say this, would be to state

> "I left three messages and have not received a response."

The difference might seem very small, but the effect is not. Both for you and the receiver of your communication. The conclusion drawn in the first example is one of negligence, intention or mean intent.

> "Don't want to call me back"

Infers something wrong. This leaves the receiver of your message wondering what is wrong with the person for whom your left the message or with you that you are so disgusting that they would not want to call you back.

I know I am blowing this up a bit, but here is the point. The first example contains emotion and added meaning, and the second does not.

"Don't want to call me back"

vs

"Not received a response".

What happens inside your brain every time you use a word with loaded meaning is that you reinforce a very subtle judgment of the situation.

AND you are doing this all of the time and in almost every situation.

Do the following:

Say: "I have not gotten a call in over three days, they must not love me anymore."

Now feel the emotion of what you just said. Make it real for yourself. Think of a time when this might have been a situation you experienced. Sit with the feelings for a few seconds.

Now say the factual version of the same scenario, "I have not gotten a call in three days from her/him."

Now feel the emotion. Unless you are mentally creating the same reaction to the first sentence in your brain, there will be a significant shift in the experience of the emotions.

We are going to discuss Judgment in a later chapter in this book. But for now, just notice that the language we use brings a subtle judgment to almost everything we say.

If we choose to say only what is factually in evidence we can give ourselves some breathing room to not create or expand our emotional responses.

"I hate her/him for what he/she said about me."

Becomes:

"She/he said things."

Then:

"Oh, my god, my life is cursed, nothing seems to go right for me."

Becomes:

*"Several challenges (opportunities) have
shown up for me recently."*

Feel the lack of emotional charge in the "factual" rather than "judgmental" statements. Without the emotion, it is much easier to move through the day. Even though something has yet to be resolved, we don't have to get caught up in the highs and lows of the emotional journey.

There is an additional side benefit to this new language approach.

We create our emotional realities.

As I have discussed earlier in this book, we author our emotional reactions. Something happens/we create an emotional response.

As we say things that have an emotional charge, we increase that emotion in our life.

I am just miserable, sad, hurt, depressed.

(you get the picture)

When we say "They won't return my calls...", Although it is more subtle, we are forwarding the emotion of hurt, anger or frustration. When we convert this language, we have the option to eliminate of minimize the impact. If we do this enough, we can substantially increase our satisfaction and happiness.

Our words create our reality.

"I will never amount to anything"

"Anything is possible"

"I am not talented in that way"

"I am capable of overcoming any challenge"

All of these phrases create a reality. They are a prediction of the future. The more often we repeat them, the more likely they will come to pass. If we instead choose to say things that predict a positive and powerful outcome, then those outcomes become more likely.

Action:

This one is very simple. But please be patient with yourself. You have practiced the habit of your speech for YEARS. Please don't expect to completely alter things overnight.

As you move through your daily routine, notice when you make statements that have an emotional component. If you are paying close attention, you may find that the vast majority of everything has emotion contained in your words.

This will make it easier to find
opportunities to do this exercise.

When you notice that you voice a statement containing emotion, stop for a moment (if appropriate) and recreate the statement in a purely factual way. This may take some practice. Once you have recreated your statement, try it on for any residual emotion. Keep revising until you can feel neutral about the statement. It may take several iterations to land on one that works.

If it is too difficult (or emotionally charged) let that one go, and wait for the next opportunity.

Make a game of this. See how many times each day you can revise your statements to become factual. You can do this with the things other people say.

You may find that easier.

Warning: Don't do this out loud, nor tell other people what you are doing. You may find people have little sense of humor with what they consider to be the "true" emotional situation.

Use caution.

Continue to do this for a minimum of 7 days. If you want a life filled with joy and freedom, continue indefinitely.

This, as with most behavior modifiers in this book is a good place to insert the NIC technology.

Comparison
is the thief
of joy

Chapter

Judgment

I'm laying on a gurney in a room in the Emergency at Sharp Memorial. On this trip I had been ushered to a room rather rapidly due to my complaint of chest pain and shortness of breath.

After the usual blood and EKG tests, there was a quiet moment before the portable chest x-ray technician was due.

After a pair of knocks and my response, in to my room walks a young male nurse who identifies himself as a representative from registration. He asks the usual questions and then asks what I do for a living? After telling him I am a coach, he asks, "what is the ONE piece of advise I would give him as a young nurse just starting his career?"

I told him "learn to live judgment free."

Since this demanded a more in depth explanation, I proceeded to spend the next 45 minutes showing him why and how.

We, as humans, judge everything. Things happen in the World and we have a judgment about all of them.

"That guy looks filthy, he must be homeless".

"She is always complaining, she must have had a bad childhood".

"I am always tripping on my words, I must be stupid".

At a glance, we draw conclusions about the people, places and things we see every day. It takes no effort. It flows from us as easily as breathing.

Human beings add meanings to everything that happens and every circumstance that our lives come across.

We see someone with different clothing,
"They are looking for attention."

We see a penny on the ground, "Today is going to be a lucky day."

Someone does not respond to our text, "They are ghosting me."

Now, notice that even as you were reading those scenarios, you may have been coming up with different meanings for the situations. Finding the penny for you may have nothing to do with luck. Perhaps you do not believe in the concept of luck.

But this only serves to further make my point. We all are adding judgments to everything in our lives, all of the time. It is automatic and instant.

These occurrences do not exist for us as judgments or even separate events. The process is simultaneous.

Penny = Luck

Weird Clothes = Attention

No Response = Ghosting

This behavior for humans happens so continuously and instantly that, in our minds the judgment and the occurrence become the same thing.

If we allow ourselves to review the situations objectively, we can see that the thing that happens is distinct from the judgment we make about it.

There is a penny on the ground

And nothing more.

What might happen if we chose to alter this behavior. What if every time we notice a judgment come up in our brain, we stop and then consider a more useful thing to make up about the given situation?

Can I even do that?

We are able to choose a more graceful option in every situation.

"He looks like he has not showered, perhaps he could use some information about social services".

"She seems to have some concerns, perhaps I can provide some solutions".

"I seem to be tripping over my words today, maybe I should cut back on the caffeine or get better sleep tonight".

My primary message here is this: We are making up the judgments about everything anyway, why not make up a judgment that empowers others and yourself?

It is up to you.

Action:

Use the NIC technology and once you have interrupted your initial judgment, create a judgment that empowers you or the person for whom you created the judgment initially or both of you. This way, you need not stop making judgments, you can simply use them to forward something rather than build barriers.

As an example:

You see someone struggling with a project at work.

In the past, you may have had a judgment about this person that they were incompetent or slow to pick up their tasks at work.

This time, you pause, take your three deep breaths and invent that they are simply missing sufficient information to complete the task. So you offer your assistance to get them past the lack of knowledge. In this instance, they grow from the experience and become a more valued member of the work team.

Go out and do this starting today.

Another form of judgment that doesn't serve us is comparison.

"Her car is nicer than mine".

"She is way smarter than me, so I will go with what she says".

When we spend our time comparing ourselves to others, we emotionally elevate or diminish ourselves, neither of which is useful.

"She has a nice car. She deserves that for her hard work."

"She seems smart, I should collaborate on this project with her."

In comparison we have another chance to elevate our self-talk and the things we say to and about others.

She is prettier than I am.

He is in better shape than I am.

Those people are lucky to have all of that wealth.

Comparison is a special kind of judgment. Not a particularly useful form, but another form nevertheless.

When we spend time judging that one thing is better or more desirable than another, we are wasting our time. You have what you have. Others have what they have and are what they are.

If you find that you wish to have something that you do not, awesome, set that intention and align your actions to acquire what you want.

When you spend your time comparing yourself and your skills or possessions, you will only create stress or resentment.

Eliminate judgment and find peace.

"To live a creative
life, we must
lose our fear of
being wrong."

- Joseph Chilton Pearce

Chapter

Being Right

How good does it feel when you are having a disagreement with someone and you both do the research and discover that YOU were right? It is a very satisfactory feeling. Warm and triumphant. Leaves you feeling great!

Now how does it feel being the one who was proven wrong. It takes a little bit of your soul. Especially if the argument was extensive and you were totally convinced that your position was just and correct.

Being right feels good. Being wrong feels bad.

Have you ever participated in a prolonged argument that got heated at some point, only to discover that even though you knew without any question you were right, that you were wrong? Did your pride get injured? Did you say things you regret having said to the other person? How would the situation have changed if you did not need to be right? Don't worry about the other person. If you had immediately stated "you are probably right about that" no matter what the reality, you would have saved a bit of time and the heated conversation and possible embarrassment.

What would your world look like if you
gave up the right to be right?

At the very least you would have more time on your hands. It takes a great deal of time to argue with others to defend your "rightness".

Even when you ARE right it may be useful to choose not to be. This could be a VERY challenging concept. You may be sitting there reading this and thinking "but if I AM right, why would I ever choose to let someone think I am wrong and they are right".

Why indeed?

It can be powerful to grant "rightness" to another person. Giving them the experience of the triumph of being right regardless of whether they are or not. Consider the emotional bridge you can create by giving them this gift. Energetically, you have granted them the upper hand in the discussion. This shifts the balance so that they are more open to you and the concepts you wish to explore.

Let's say for the purpose of this exercise that you are having a disagreement with a loved one. The topic is not important as long as you can imagine something that you are on opposite sides about.

You have now spent a few minutes in conflict defending your two positions. You can feel the tension building as you both feel strongly about you opinion. (or even the facts as you perceive them)

Things are escalating and you can feel you face flushing with blood as you become frustrated or angry that they cannot seem to grasp the truth of your position.

Then, you pause. You listen to them for a minute considering their position. You still feel that they are wrong, but this time you do something unexpected.

You agree that they are right.

You simply state "you are right about that, I can see that now."

You feel the energy in the space dissipate. The air in the room seems lighter. You can head the conversation in another direction or stop altogether since you have completed the argument with the recognition that they are right.

For now, the topic is over and resolved. Perhaps at a later time you can reconvene the discussion when you have materials to support your claims.

Or maybe you can walk away complete because the topic of discussion was truly not that important and in retrospect, served no real purpose.

And what does it cost you?

Nothing.

If you walk away from the conversation right or wrong, the only difference is how you make yourself feel. So perhaps you attain an increase in self-esteem by being right; but you can give that to yourself at any time irrespective of your rightness or wrongness.

As you progress through the next seven
days, practice giving up being right.

Catch yourself in arguments and conversations being positional about something. Then say to the other person, "You are probably right about that". Then smile. (Avoid sounding sarcastic. Be authentic when you tell them they are right) Soon you will notice even before you have begun to argue, that you can give grace to the other person.

Notice how happy you have made them.

You may have practiced your whole life being right. Start practicing the rest of your life not needing to be right. Your friends and acquaintances will notice the difference.

You will need to be sincere in granting rightness to another. It will not be effective if you say sarcastically "I guess you are right."

You must be authentic about allowing them to win the right/wrong battle.

You may even notice that you gain more persuasive advantage by releasing your need to be correct in a given situation. This is an interesting dynamic. In a life where you have more often argued for being right in disagreements, you will notice an energy shift when you begin to allow other the grace to be right. (EVEN WHEN THEY ARE WRONG) Granting them their "rightness" puts then "on their heels" a bit. You now have a chance to make a persuasive appeal (on a different topic) and gain some ground.

You will also notice the freedom and joy of granting others the right to be right. In so doing, you can reduce and in some cases eliminate the tension and stress of your typical day.

For some of you this concept may prove almost impossible. Many of you have cultivated a life where being right about most things is your way of staying ahead and in some cases, advancing. I am not saying you never get to be right, I am saying you get to choose when to be and when not to be. The power for living comes from making a choice.

Both positions provide you an advantage at different times.

Just take this exercise on for the next seven days and explore the opportunity of choosing to be right or choosing not to be.

Action:

Use the NIC technology to notice and interrupt times that you feel the need to be right. Create a new outcome for disagreements with others.

Action two:

You may find this one more enjoyable and easier to accomplish.

Start to notice when other people around you sacrifice something they want in order to be right. If you are paying close attention you will begin to notice that others (maybe you too) will give up love, safety, relationships, health and nearly every other thing in life in order to be right.

Once you notice this behavior, start to conjecture on alternative outcomes. How would the life of these people be altered if they simply gave up being right?

How would yours?

People will Love you.

People will Hate you.

**And none of it will have
anything to do with you.**

Chapter

Gossip

A definition for gossip is having a conversation about someone with someone else who cannot make a difference.

This behavior is not only a waste of time, but it stands a very good chance of resulting in friction between you and the person you are talking about or even to. If you gossip enough, you will alienate everyone around you except the people who thrive on gossip.

Gossip is a huge waste of your time.

Remember that your assessment of anyone is colored by your past and your experiences. The first thing you should do is mistrust the conclusions you arrive at regarding that person. Most likely, nothing needs to be said at all.

Take stock, would the things you wish to say result in benefit for the other person or your relationship with them. Is what you wish to tell them a contribution? If so, go directly to them and let them know your concerns.

Start the conversation with an expression of your care for them or an apology. Like: I am sorry to take your time on this, but I wanted to share my observations from the other day.

Be clear to them that these are your opinions only, and that you don't want them to hear your comments as true.

Just as your opinions.

Then tell them what you wish to say. Do this without and expectation for change or acknowledgment. You have provided them with the information from which they can benefit. That is all there is to do.

If they disagree with your conclusions, thank them for considering your input. It is not important that they agree or even agree to change. You are there to impart helpful information.

Nothing else.

Consider if there is ANY value in what you have to say to this person. I am sure they have lived a useful life up to this moment. Is your motive for having this conversation with them to empower them or to make you feel good about being right about something?

You can practice avoiding gossip by simply enacting the exercise from the second chapter. (NIC) You can also enlist the help of the people around you to hold you to your new desired behavior. Ask your co-workers and close friends to stop you if you begin to engage in gossip. (You may end up having an impact on them and the amount of gossip in which they engage)

Also, when you are having conversations with others, let them know that you would prefer to disengage if anyone is going to gossip. This may save you getting tangled up in the complicity later once the gossip is found out. In social settings, you can also quietly walk away from groups who are gossiping. You do not need to be right about your choice to avoid gossip. Neither do you need to lord you new found behavior as superior to others. These are choices you are making for YOUR life and YOUR empowerment. The point, here, has nothing to do with being better than anyone else. The point is to move your evolution forward.

Consider the savings in time and efficiency. Start to track all of the time you and others spend on gossip. Now think of what could be accomplished productively with that amount of time.

It is far easier to be happy when you are not spending time worrying about what might make it back to your friends or what others are saying about you.

Pay attention to your conversations in general. Is something created when you engage in conversation? Are your conversations generative or simply oscillating your vocal chords? Make it a practice to evaluate all of your conversations to determine if something new is created.

Be generous with yourself.

You have been creating the you that you are right now for years. Perhaps even decades. While most of this creation has happened unconsciously, it has still happened then repeated, then happened and repeated endlessly.

You have been an expert in creating the you, you are right now.

It is said that practice makes perfect. Well, you have practiced you current behaviors and responses for tens or even hundreds of thousands of iterations. You have created yourself to be the master of being who you are.

Consider that it may take some time and some practice to change your behaviors to new desired ones.

The NIC tool is designed to be repeated over and over and over again, until the new desired behavior takes over the old habit.

Remember that you are physically altering the pathways in your brain.

Be patient with yourself to allow this evolutionary change.

Show respect even for people
who don't deserve it.

Not as measure of
their character but as
a measure of yours.

Chapter

Stop Complaining

If you are complaining to or about yourself, you are wasting your time and not moving anything forward. If you are complaining to other people then you are wasting two people's time and energy.

Seem selfish?

When there is something in your world that is not working as well as it can, act to resolve it. If you cannot resolve it, report it to someone who can and move on.

Don't waste time complaining about it.

Have you ever stopped and counted the amount of time you spend complaining? For most of us, it includes a significant portion of our lives. Reclaiming this time could allow you to be more effective and even provide you more time to do the things you enjoy. Generally, we are happier when we are not complaining.

A definition for complaining is:

Expressing dissatisfaction or annoyance about something.

Notice that this definition says nothing about taking action or resolving the situation. Generally, the intention of complaining is to gain someone else's agreement about a situation, event or person that you have an issue with. Sometimes even "constructive criticism" is merely a mask for another opportunity to complain.

What would be available if you spent the time you currently use to complain and instead took action to resolve the problem?

Time to invoke the chapter two exercise. Notice, interrupt, create.

As part of your process to end your complaints, as you successfully reduce them over time, notice how the people around you start to see you and expect you to be. Is there a newly found respect from them concerning you? Have you become a doer rather than a talker?

Often people will notice the changes in you and even comment on them. This phenomenon is something that can help you rise to your newly established behavior. Once you start to develop your new habits, folks will learn to expect them from you and often mention when you slip.

You can even engage the people around you that you trust to help you evolve into the new behaviors and the person you wish to be.

Remember back when you were young? Did your parents ever tell you to stop whining? Did they tell you that there is no whining allowed? Did you find that it became more effective to simply make a request for the things that you wanted?

Complaining is the adult version of whining. (Adult?)

You may find that it takes some focus to notice complaining in yourself.

We often are reluctant to see our own shortcomings.

We discussed conversation that does not generate anything in the last chapter. Start to review all of your conversations. Is something being generated? Are you simply complaining?

Sometimes the best alternative is to get quiet and simply listen. You may find that you can accomplish far more with silence than talking.

Perhaps this is worth exploring.

Remember that your complaints are not about what is true or what is so. You are complaining about what you have made up about someone else or a situation. Are you correct? Are you sure? Does it matter?

Remember our chapter on giving up being right or even your right to be right?

If you are willing to give up being right about the thing you are complaining about, you may find there is no complaint to be had.

You have a choice to make in every situation. If something or someone is not the way you would prefer, and you are not just making it up, you can either change the situation or accept it. Either choice will take an action to alter your perspective.

Complaining will not accomplish anything.

The next time you notice that you have a complaint about someone or something, touch your wrist and create an action to fix the situation or engage the person and find a way to help them.

If there is no wind, row.

Latin Proverb

Chapter

Slow Down

Abraham Lincoln is quoted as having said; *"Give me six hours to chop down a tree and I will spend the first four sharpening the ax."*

Our World continues to move at an increasingly more rapid pace. The work world honors and respects anyone with a schedule that is packed with tasks from dusk to dawn. It is often considered a badge of honor to be "too busy" to consider even one more item added to your week.

Do you find yourself proud of your 70-90-hour work week?

Do you feel superior to those around you who only spend 40 hours per week working?

What about in traffic?

Do you find yourself weaving in and out of lanes to make sure you get to your destination as rapidly as possible? Do traffic jams upset you because you need to get somewhere right now?

It seems perfectly normal to adhere to all of these or at least some of these behaviors. We as a culture tend to reward or hold these traits in high esteem.

Yet if we want to be accurate, precise and happy, we may want to slow down a bit. If we lose the manic pace, we can get things done correctly the first time, rather than have to go back and correct mistakes that we made due to being in a hurry.

It is also easier to remain peaceful and happy if we reject the concept that we must always be in a rush. If we allow ourselves to focus on the task at hand, we can get the task completed more accurately and more rapidly than if we are distracted by the multitude of tasks looming before us.

How many times have you forgotten or skipped over a task because you were worried about some future task in your calendar?

Allow yourself some grace. Let your mind slow down and focus on your task at hand. And ONLY the task at hand.

Use a calendar planning tool to capture your tasks on a day-to-day basis so you can stop waisting time worrying about if you got everything done. Place anything that will occupy a block of time on your calendar. Do not only list the items that pertain to your "work" week or seem important enough to be on your calendar. If you intend to spend an amount of time on any given task, put it in your calendar. If it exists, put it on your calendar. If it need never actually happen, don't bother.

Use the brain retraining tool in chapter 2 to NOTICE when you are in a hurry during your day. Then INTERRUPT the behavior and finally CREATE a peaceful more focused way of being instead.

With enough repetition, you will be able to eliminate the stress of always being behind and you will be capable of focused, efficient implementation of the things you need to do in your daily life.

If you are always manic in traffic, develop a practice to leave for your destinations earlier. Relax and focus on the drive. (and only the drive)

If you find yourself rushing through your morning routine every day, Get up 30 minutes earlier and take your time to enjoy each of your morning tasks. Focus on each task as it comes.

Be mindful of the task at hand.

If you are a blur in your workplace, set up your calendar at the beginning of the week to include all of your tasks in a precise schedule of events with alarms. This way you can move from task to task knowing that your week is taken care of since you have done the planning in advance.

Give yourself an hour of unallocated time toward the end of your work day to catch back up on any task that was interrupted during your day. This will also give you a spot to get any lingering task complete that have been stealing mental space from you.

If you stop inventing that everything is immediate and urgent, you can give yourself space to slow down and increase your effectiveness.

Gain some self-esteem and stop letting others dictate your pace.

Move with tranquility in the World.

Be willing to walk alone.

Many who started with you won't finish with you.

Chapter

Kind vs Nice

Do you consider yourself a nice person? Do you provide help to other when they need it? Are you always one of the first to offer to volunteer when some project or task needs to be done?

Good for you.

Are you finding yourself saying nice things to people because you don't want to hurt their feelings? Do you agree with the group simply to avoid additional conflict?

The definition of the word kind (as an adjective) is: "having or showing a friendly, generous, and considerate nature."

The word comes from the Old English - gecynde "natural, native"; in Middle English the earliest use of the word meant "well born or well bred", hence "well-disposed by nature, courteous, gentle, benevolent".

The definition of the word nice (as an adjective) is: "pleasant; agreeable; satisfactory."

The origins of nice include from Middle English (meaning "stupid"), from Latin - nescius "ignorant".

You know plenty of people who are really "nice". They may even seem to be door mats. Do they let others get away with anything in order to remain nice? Are you one of those people?

Being kind may actually show up as being direct and honest with someone. Will you be nice and let someone continue to make mistakes, or will you be kind to them and tell them how to avoid those mistakes in the future.

You may find that it takes a bit of courage to make a difference for another. It takes no courage to be nice.

What would the kind thing to do be? What could you say with kindness that would propel someone else forward.

Most importantly, are you being nice to yourself and avoiding changes that would make life more effective in order to not make waves?

Treat yourself and others with kindness. Happiness is easier to experience if you do.

Kindness can sometimes feel like being mean or rude.

"Aunt Nancy, that is a lovely hat and it brings out your eyes."

The preceding statement could be an example of being nice as well as kind. If the hat is disgusting, you might be saving your Aunt some awkward moments later by letting her know about the hat. Although, if she is highly invested in her hat, it costs nothing to feed her pride a bit.

There are other situations where being nice may cost the recipient embarrassment or even safety. In this instance, choose kindness and tell the truth to avoid the impact for them later.

Be kind to others and yourself.

Don't look back

You're not going that way

Chapter

Be Present

All you ever have is now.

You cannot operate or change the past. You can put it away and learn from the lessons generated by your prior experiences. I strongly recommend that you do whatever it takes to leave your past in the past where it belongs.

At the end of each year, I undertake a process to actively place my past experiences in the past. I take out my journal and make a list of the regrets or what I consider, mistakes from the prior twelve months. I then write the life lesson that came out of each of these occurrences. I make sure to go over the list a few times in order to ensure my list is comprehensive.

I take the page from my journal (you may wish to use a tablet of some sort in order not to ruin your journal)

Outside, somewhere safe, I take the page from my journal and set it on fire. While it is burning, out loud, I declare myself complete with all of the history and lessons learned.

Then, I list out all of the triumphs and times I succeeded in the prior twelve months. I allow myself to celebrate each of the triumphs as I write them down. Then I burn that page as well.

Now that my past year is complete, any time I feel a reaction creeping up on me that belongs in my past, I am able to move past this and make decisions in the present time having completed my past.

Another way to be present, is to practice Mindfulness. This concept has become popular recently. The origins of mindfulness come from Buddhism. But the concept is useful regardless of from whence it came.

To be present is to be focused on your task at hand and only the task at hand. For instance, if you are sitting down, focus on sitting down. Feel the flex of your leg muscles as you squat to sit in the chair. Feel the release of the muscle tension as your weight is taken up by your gluteus maximus. Feel the heat/cold of the chair surface as you lean back.

In the same way, when you are at your desk doing a task on your computer, focus on only doing that task. Turn off your phone, alarms, distractions of any sort and simply focus on the task at hand.

Eating your cereal? Same type of focus.

Walking down the street? Only focus on walking.

When we practice being tuned in to the moment we occupy, we are more effective in doing what we are doing.

This also makes us set aside the past and anything we have made up so that it cannot affect our mindset or efficiency.

Dwelling in the future can have a similar impact on our daily lives. I am not saying you should not plan or set goals, just that after doing so, stop WISHING your future was here and take actions.

When you are planning/creating your future, be totally present to the activity of creating. Like any other thing you can be present to, remember that you are inventing a future you intend to realize. Don't let past based evidence or worry, impact the future you are creating.

Use the exercise from chapter two to notice when you are not being present, interrupt the action and substitute focus and presence of mind.

You will discover that life is much easier to live if you choose to do so one moment at a time. If you have found life to be overwhelming, this is the action for you to take right now, in the present.

Negative emotions are a function of the past or future almost exclusively.

When we are present, we release the power that time has on our lives.

Think about it.

Fear is based upon something that may happen in the future. Regret is based upon something in the past. Anger is about something that has or will happen.

If you are in traffic and you see a car racing toward you in your rear view mirror, it is appropriate and wise to react accordingly. The fear in you creates chemical reactions the bring clarity and power to your body.

As soon as the impact happens and everyone has come to a stop, it has become time to let the fear, anger, regret or whatever other emotions you are experiencing go.

Now is the time to get present and deal with the steps of collecting the information necessary to deal with the accident. When you are able to become mindful even in stressful situations, you will find yourself making better decisions and able to resume your day effectively.

There is no value in expressing your anger. There is tremendous value in being level headed and composed. All of this is possible from being precisely present.

The one who falls and stands up is so much stronger than the one who never fell.

Chapter

Celebrate Your Wins

Generally, we don't have any problem punishing ourselves for the things we screw up or mistakes we make.

What is more rare is to take note of the successes we achieve or celebrate our wins.

The things we send more energy to, in our worlds, are the things that expand the most. Make a mistake? The more you bemoan the situation and punish yourself, the more the mistake and others like it expand.

The best dog trainers have discovered that punishing the animal for mistakes during potty training is less effective than ignoring the mistakes and praising the successes.

This works the same for people.

If we celebrate the things that we do well or win at, it will expand the energy around winning. The end result is that we will win more often and succeed more often.

The action to take in, this regard, is to notice when we punish ourselves and interrupt the punishing behavior.

At the same time, celebrate every time we win. I don't mean that you should book a sea cruse every time you are on time for work, but even a quick fist pump expands the energy of the win.

As you go through your day, find things to celebrate. Quick validations should be enough. Then each evening, with your journal, write down a few of your favorite successes of the day. Then, the next time you go to dinner or take a road trip, choose what wins you are celebrating by doing so.

Over time you will create a habit of self-congratulations and expand the parts of life that make you happy.

Consider that doing the same for others (kids, spouses, co-workers, etc.) will have the same impact. You can guide the direction and expand positive behaviors with a simple "great job".

A key to happiness is letting
each situation be what it is rather
than what you think it should
be, then making the best of it.

Chapter

Acceptance

Accepting things as they are is a great way to eliminate stress and anxiety in your life.

Have you ever noticed how things are the way they are? You have the amount of money that you have. You have the relationship that you have. You have the family that you have. And so forth.

"I wish I had more money".

"I wish I had a better relationship".

"I want a family that gets along".

Wouldn't it be great if that was all it took to accomplish the things in our lives?

Let's use lack of money as the example here. "I don't have enough money to pay my bills".

This statement may be factual. To find out, add up all of the places you made money last month and come up with a total. Now, add up all of your expenses from last month and get a total. If the first total is greater than the second total, you have enough money to pay your bills. If the reverse is true, then you do not have enough money to pay your bills.

Either way, you now have the facts.

You may notice that there is some kind of emotion related to the concept that you do not have enough money to pay your bills. Is it fear, frustration, terror, anger or stress? Whatever emotion you have associated with this situation is a result of your particular experiences and filters.

What is the result of the emotion you feel about this situation? Do you get depressed, go hide, lash out? Whatever your reaction to lack of money is, it takes and uses energy.

Visualize, for a moment, the following scenario: You, and another person are standing face-to-face on a flat surface. Now we instruct the other person to push on your hands with theirs with the intention of pushing you off of your feet. Your instructions are to remain on your feet.

The person leans in and starts pushing on you. At first you simply meet their energy with enough return pressure to remain standing.

But then they apply more pressure. You find that you need to respond with an increase in your energy to push back or resist falling over.

This can continue for some time until you fall over or the person exhausts themselves while trying to displace you.

Notice that the more they exert, the more pressure you need to respond with.

Emotional energy works the same way. The more you resist the way things are ("I wish I had more money") the more they stay the same. Every time you complain about your situation, every time you worry about your income, every time you tell other people about your plight, you are building the energetic pressure against finding the solution to your situation.

Let's go back to our pushing scenario. The instructions are the same to both of you. But this time, as the other person leans in to push you, You simply step to the side. The other person either moves past you or falls forward in the space you left.

Notice that the amount of energy you expend is minimal. The amount of energy to step aside. Also note that regardless of the amount of opposing energy (their pushing forward to topple you) it requires no more energy on your part.

It is the same way with resisting your emotions or situations.

When you ACCEPT your lot in life, you allow your situation to change. You stop building a wall of resistance that keeps you in the same place. "I have the amount of money that I have". "I have the relationship that I have". I have the family that I have".

DO NOT misinterpret what I am saying as resignation or giving up. Accepting your situation is simply an acknowledgment of the way things currently are. With the resistant energy eliminated, you can now affect change to alter your current reality.

Once you are willing to accept that "I have the amount of money that I have", then you are free to invent the next action. "I will reduce the bills that I have so that the amount of money that I have is sufficient". "I will ask my boss for a raise so that I can afford my current lifestyle". "I will find a new job that I love and pays me better".

Without your emotional resistance, anything is now possible.

How does this affect your past? How effective have you been at changing your past no matter how much energy you have given to it? You may have noticed that what has happened, has already happened and no matter how much you wish it had not, you have the past that you have.

Have you ever made a big mistake and then wish you had not? Have you ever been run into by another car and thought, if I had left one minute later this would not have happened? You did what you did, the car hit you. ACCEPT and move on.

Carrying around the baggage of all of your prior missed steps and unfortunate occurrences is a heavy burden. No wonder we stoop over as we get older. Consider how much easier and happier life can be if we leave this baggage behind?

In order to live a happy life, we need to accept things more and more rapidly and take actions consistent with the future we envision for ourselves.

And others

Are there people in your life that you would love to change?

Does someone drink too much?

Is someone too bossy?

Is someone too loud/quiet?

How many times can you see that you have solutions for other folks in the World.

"If they could just understand, they would vote differently."

"They should do what I do so they would have a better life."

What could become possible for these people if you accepted them for who and how they are?

What would become possible for YOU?

You might discover that folks have more freedom to evolve when there is less external pressure for them to conform to your view for them.

Perhaps they are on a journey to somewhere amazing. It will be easier for them to get there if they are allowed the space to fail and change.

People come into this existence with a pathway in mind. They generally are unaware of what this path is. But it has already been largely defined. It is a particular arrogance to think that you have a better plan for other folks. I would contend that it is a life long exploration for each of us, just to discover our own journey. Who has time to direct the pathway for other people?

Do you want to be happy?

Let go of what's gone, be grateful for what remains and look forward to what is coming.

Chapter

Gratitude

Are you grateful for all of the accomplishments and experiences of your life?

Are you grateful for all of the challenges of your life?

I am not referring to things and experiences granted you by others. Also not the challenges that have been inflicted upon you.

I am talk about the life you have constructed, both challenging and rewarding. You authored all of it one way or another.

Gratitude could be considered the next level of acceptance. As you saw in the last chapter, one way to move resistant energy out of the way of your forward progress is to accept the things and the past that you have. Gratitude can be used in the same way, but on steroids.

"FUCK", I yelled very loudly! That really hurt!

I looked down and saw the yellow paddles moving away from my chest. I looked past them to see the laughing face of my cardiologist. I instantly remembered that a few moments ago I had faded to black. I quickly reasoned that I had died and they had to shock me back to life.

I thanked the Doc for keeping me around.

He told me, "you're welcome".

I lay there thinking how interesting it was that what had started as a relatively normal day, had progressed to one of life and death quite literally.

I reflected, as I lay there with wires and tubes coming out of me about what had just transpired.

The cardiologist was discussing that he intended to keep me in the hospital for a bit while they sought the reason behind the heart attack and how to avoid another. I agreed that would be a reasonable expectation.

As the room cleared to just the nurse taking my vitals, I was able to reflect upon what had just transpired.

I found myself grateful for the heart attack.

Truly Grateful.

I could see that having lived through it, I had an amazing new appreciation for my purpose for being here on this planet. I had started to write this book just a few months before this heart attack, but I could see in that moment, my renewed purpose and inspiration for why I am here.

As soon as I was out of the hospital I took up the writing of the book and my coaching with renewed vigor and commitment.

Everything that happens in our lives is intended to be either a lesson or a triumph. If the occurrence is not one you would like to see happen again, it is a lesson. If the occurrence is one you would like to experience over and over, it is a triumph.

So choose to learn or celebrate, this is why things happen.

I am sure you have heard the phrase "Everything happens for a reason". There you go, now you know at least one or two of the reasons.

Action:

Look back at the major events of your life. Make a two-column list. In the first column list the events that you would rather had not repeated themselves. In the second column, list the lesson you learned from those events. Don't spend any time wondering if the lesson you wrote down is the right lesson. You are making it up either way.

DO, however, make up a lesson that empowers you or provides you something to move your life path forward. Remember that you are making up ALL of it, so make up something that empowers you!

You are inventing the lesson. Make sure to invent it to your benefit.

Now make a two-column list for the triumphs in your life. Write the triumph in column one and in the second column write what you did (or will do) to celebrate the win.

Next, start celebrating.

Forgiveness doesn't excuse their behavior.

Forgiveness prevents their behavior from destroying your heart.

Chapter

Forgiveness

Anger and resentment are punishments you give yourself for something someone else did.

Are you holding on to some resentment or anger from your past?

Is it a friend or relative?

A former co-worker or employer?

If this does not apply to you, think of a friend of yours that is harboring some anger or resentment that is getting in the way of their happiness.

Do you remember what the issue was that started the anger?

Is the issue still happening?

Has it been a long time since the issue happened?

Was the thing that happened a BIG deal?

Do you think that they did it on purpose? Was it an accident?

Did they do or say something mean?

Did they hurt you?

Did they hurt someone you love?

Is it still happening?

If it is, take action to end the activity. Engage the authorities, have a conversation with the person to get them to stop. If they won't extricate them from your life.

THEN

Forgive them. It costs you nothing. Nothing. That argument that is talking in your head is just your human being paying attention to what society wants for you. If you are finished punishing yourself for something someone else did, forgive them. Stop carrying around the burden of resentment and anger. The only one who is being punished is YOU.

Then forgive yourself. That is free too. Perhaps you have a complicit role in what took place, perhaps you don't. It really does not matter. At the very least you can forgive yourself for carrying this burden for such a long time.

Then keep doing it. Maybe even get up each morning and forgive yourself for everything. Then start your day.

You can choose to reconcile with this person or not. You forgiveness for them or you requires no ones participation but your own. Even if this person is no longer alive, forgive them and yourself.

Action:

What is the most embarrassing or guilt invoking event in your past?

Write it down on a piece of paper.

Read it out loud to yourself in the mirror.

Do it again.

Now do it again.

Repeat 25 times.

Are you sick of the exercise?

Good.

What you wrote is no longer happening. It is in your past. Please allow it to stay there.

Take the paper outside. Find a container in which to burn the paper. Put the paper in the container.

Light the paper on fire.

As you watch the paper burn and turn into smoke, forgive yourself.

Keep forgiving until the paper is gone completely.

Dump the ashes in the yard (responsively)

OK, now you are done with that piece of your history.

DONE.

If the thoughts of that particular event encroach upon your life again, repeat this exercise until they don't.

*Stop letting
people who
do so little
for you,
control
so much of
your mind,
feelings
and emotions.*

Chapter

Learn to Say No

Are you the type of person who has difficulty saying no when asked to volunteer or contribute to others, or for that matter in most situations?

Consider that the short-term satisfaction of "doing good" can quickly become tiresome and burdensome to your already full schedule.

You can do far better, if you learn to say no and save everyone the complaining and resistance in the future.

Have you ever walked into a store and had the clerk say something like "may I help you with something?"

Then you respond, "no, I am just looking."

And they respond, "Looking for what? I am sure I can help you find what you need."

Well trained sales people are trained to work with whatever you provide them in order to address your objections and ultimately get all of your objections solved so you are left with a yes to their product.

Here is what I mean.

You: "I don't see the type of car I am looking for on your lot."

Salesperson: "We have access to any car in a 100 mile radius. What features are you looking for?"

You: "I was hoping for a red one with a soft top."

Salesperson: "Let's go inside and I can check on my computer."

You: "Well I don't think I can afford one anyway."

Salesperson: "We can finance anyone and I am sure we can find a payment that works for you."

Etc.

Now how is this scenario different if your response is simply "no".

Salesperson: "Is there something I can show you today?"

You: "No."

Salesperson: Is there a color or some special equipment you are looking for?"

You: "No."

It is hard to take the conversation anywhere productive if there is no objection to respond to.

We, as humans tend to want to fill in awkward spaces in conversation. If the other person does not fill the space with words, there is an energetic want or need to fill the space.

Are you one of those people who want to do good everywhere you can in the World?

Well, STOP THAT!

If you say yes to every charity and cause on the planet, you will not be able to do a good job for any of them.

You do not have to have a "good" reason for you to say no. Use no without any reason. Not "No I just don't have the time." Simply say "no" or "no thank you".

I am speaking from experience. Practice saying NO first to every request to volunteer or contribute that comes your way. After the no, and not the no because, you can take some time to consider if the project fits in your schedule and fits in your desire to make a difference. The organization will always accept a yes after the no.

When someone
tells you it
can't be done,
it's more
a reflection of
their limitations,
not yours.

Chapter

Stop Listening to What "They" Say

Who the heck are "they" anyway.

What I am referring to are the times you hear from people around you, things like:

"You have to love yourself before you can love someone else"

"Flu season starts in October"

"You will never succeed at anything until you find your passion".

We hear these types of platitudes all of the time. Sometimes we hear them on TV by virtue of commercials or even in TV programs.

Sometimes we hear our friends or those around us say things like these. When someone is offering advice to us, "they say" type comments come up frequently.

Let's start with, "who are they"?

Is there a room somewhere filled with arbiters of truth that publish these sayings to benefit all of humanity? Is there some agency that collects opinions from all people in order to supply us with majority wisdom?

The answer to these questions is, obviously, no.

Yet someone says something to us that "they" say and we take it as truthful.

Most human beings use this device because they think that if they themselves were to offer up some bit of advice, it would not carry the same weight as if "they" said it. They are right to believe this because, most of the time, that is exactly what happens.

This is not to say that some of these tidbits of advice are not useful, or even insightful.

It just is not sufficient to accept things simply because a large number of people have said them.

Think for yourself!

When someone offers you the wisdom of "they", stop and question it.

Does it apply to you?

Do you agree with it?

Can you take some value from it?

Is it ridiculous?

Put these slices of advice to the test. Try them on for size and realize that you need not accept of apply them to your life unles you derive some measure of value.

I would be particularly suspect when someone offers you "TRUTH".

Truth can be situational, individual and faulty. Is there scientific support for the "truth". Simply that it is a commonly held belief, is not sufficient reason to accept it.

The more you question, the more you will build a powerful base for your choices and the actions you take in life.

Choose what works for you.

Collect as much information as you can, and then, choose your pathway.

*Make sure you don't start
seeing yourself through
the eyes of those who
don't value you.*

*Know your worth
even if they don't.*

Chapter

What Do Other People Think of Me

Who cares? The response to "who cares" is almost everyone. We all, for the most part, are concerned about how we are perceived in the World. Do we look good, fit in, say the right things or hang with the right people?

What if we did not have to waist time and energy on these considerations?

What people say to you or others about you has very little or nothing to do with you.

Remember back in this book where we discussed that people add meaning to everything? They do it about each other as well.

The meanings or judgments those around you come from THEIR past and experiences, not from you. In a room with ten people, there will be eleven evaluations drawn about you. Each of the ten people and you. Which ones are right? Yours? Theirs?

How about none of the above?

Even you and your assessments are colored by your past experiences of yourself. More importantly, who cares? If the intention of the meeting is to get feedback on your behaviors and character, then perhaps you can take what is said, learn the lessons from the group and make decisions from there. If that is not the point of the meeting, move on.

We often spend far too much time hurting, anxious or stopped by the opinions of others. If our goal in life is to be happy, then why not make up stuff about you that is inspiring and empowering?

We are making the stuff up anyway.

Scenario: You just got home from work. At lunch you went to eat with a handful of co-workers. During the conversation you are told that you are quiet and don't really fit in with the group. Later that afternoon, the boss calls you in and asks you to pay better attention to details and expects you to improve in the near future or else.

When you get home from work you ask your significant other about the information you gathered during that day, and they affirm that you DO tend to be a bit distracted.

You spend the next two hours both reflecting on the changes you need to make in your behaviors and how to demonstrate to your boss (and your significant other) your renewed focus and diligence.

Scenario 2: Everything happens as in the above scenario, except you leave lunch and realize that nothing said there had anything to do with you. After your boss meeting you resolve to be more present to your work day and life in general. You then take on practices of Mindfulness.

At home you celebrate your day with your significant other and go to dinner for the celebration.

YOU

are your only

limit.

Chapter

Created Life

You are creating your life all of the time. Most of the time you are not aware that you are doing so.

"That is way over my head".

"I can't possibly do that, it is way too difficult for me".

"I will never amount to anything".

"I feel so depressed".

You are creating your future every time you say these things. Notice that it is a future that you may not actually wish to have, but you are creating it anyway.

Consider that now that you know you are creating your future, you could take control of the things that you say such that you end up creating a future that fulfills on you goals and aspirations.

"I can accomplish anything."

"Today I will complete that project at work."

"I will find the spouse of my dreams this month."

And so on.

You are still creating your future. This time you are aware of the future you are putting into place. So, this time, you are inventing an outcome that is powerful and intentional.

With this in mind, consider that each morning when you wake up and prepare for your day, instead of lamenting how cold it is and how you would like to simply stay under your blankets and stay ward, that instead you can pivot your feet to the floor and declare (out loud if you wish) the amazing day full of successes and accomplishments you are about to experience.

What have you got to lose?

What you you accomplish?

Action:

Use the NIC technology to notice when you are creating a future that diminishes you.

Interrupt these situations by touching your wrist.

Take you three deep cleansing breaths.

Create a powerful, fulfilling future.

Create empowering statements that put into existence that future you would like to see happen.

Start to notice when you not only say these things, but also when you allow others to create these diminishing futures and you merely accept them.

Stop them. Interrupt them. Say out load a future that expands you and creates the future you want.

Start doing this in EVERY situation.

Watch your life become ever more AMAZING!

*There is no
path to
Happiness:
Happiness is
the Path.*

Buddha

Chapter

Manifest Happiness

Go ahead and do all of the things you already know how to do. Surround yourself with people that "make" you happy. Do activities that "make" you happy. Etc.

If you do not know what makes you happy, I have an exercise for you.

Create an adventure for yourself. Make a list of things you know that you enjoy. Do some work here and really think about the things you add to your list. Do you truly enjoy that activity or do you only do it to facilitate others? Kids, spouse, significant other Facebook friends?

After you have taken enough time (a couple weeks) creating this list, make another list in the next column. This list should be activities that you are not sure about, or other people have told you about but you have never tried them.

Over the next month make a concerted effort to try each of the activities in your list. Take more time as needed to accommodate the length of your list.

If at all possible, experience the activity alone. During and at the end of the event, take on the role of a critic. Evaluate your experience from positives and negatives, joy and misery. Overall, did you enjoy the activity? Would you put it in your top ten?

Was the event a flop? Was it 2 or 3 hours you will never get back? Did you like doing the activity or not?

Create a spreadsheet or a journal page with two columns. List the activities that you truly enjoyed in one column and the things you would rather avoid in the other.

When choosing to participate in events in the future, choose as often as possible, activities from the like column.

Make this exercise a lifelong project!

Go into every event in your life as the evaluator of the experience. It is not important or significant which way you go with the activity. Continue to add to your columns in your spreadsheet/journal.

Whatever you do, don't start to make up that it matters if you like or dislike an event. Your evaluations belong to you. You do not need to be right about your conclusions. Certainly, don't argue with anyone for your position. It is completely irrelevant if you like or don't like doing things. The point here is to do a specific exploration to discover the things and activities that keep you happy.

Once you have taken enough time to explore these things, choose activities from your like list as often as possible.

The final step in your happiness is to specifically create your world to be a happy space.

Make your first activity of the day to be creating your day in your head to be a series of happy events.

Find a spot that is quiet and comfortable. This activity need only take five minutes, but take more time if it pleases you.

Quiet your thoughts. Focus on the white noise, the quiet or environmental hum that exists everywhere.

Once your mind is quiet, go through your day. Think about each task or event you have scheduled or you would like to do. Create in your mind the most positive outcome for that activity. Visualize each event and "see" it in your head going the best possible way.

Then get up and go about your day.

Pause during your day to reflect on how well your day is going, or what lessons can you take away from the things that did not unfold as well as you would have liked.

Manifestation is simply the act of creating or requesting a future for yourself.

Every time you utter a sentence that starts with I want, or I wish, you are manifesting.

It does not matter if you are sending your request to the Universe or, if you prefer, the deity of your choice.

Prayer is just another form of manifestation.

Be cognizant of the future you put out into the Universe. Create amazing and fulfilling things. Then let go and allow the Universe to bring them to you. You may discover that the Universe does not provide them when or how you had imagined that it would.

But generally, you will get the things that you need.

Trust yourself and the Universe to provide. Without resistance.

The more and more often you take on manifesting, the more and more often you will have the things you desire.

The happier you will be.

*Life would
be tragic if
it weren't
so funny.*

Chapter

Be Happy, Be Human

You can see that it is up to you.

You have the capability to design your life or even modify your life to be happy, anytime, anywhere.

There is a pitfall waiting for you that you may not have considered.

I want you to reach over and gently pinch your left arm. What did you feel? Was it skin, flesh, muscle? Regardless, you should have found something over there to touch. This is because you inhabit a human body.

A skin bag.

This may seem obvious, however, It is actually remarkable.

Without going too far in depth about it, (topic for another book) you chose at some point to come here and inhabit the very human body you now find yourself within.

Your human designed your emotions and reactions as it progressed in life.

If you consider your life as good, bad, useful, useless, successful, or a failure, GOOD.

It is less important what you have done so far with your life, than what you do from now on. When you die, you can then reflect and decide if you are pleased or not pleased with your outcome.

I have spent the bulk of this book providing tools and information so you can choose Happiness.

This begs the question; is it better or worse to experience happiness all of the time? Am I a failure if I do not succeed at being happy 24/7?

I have the tools, why can't I make it work each and every time?

Now we circle back to the information you verified a few minutes ago.

YOU ARE HUMAN.

Sadness, fear, anger, depression are all human traits. Most all humans experience these things quite often. It is not Wrong to have these experiences. It may be useful to experience these things from time to time.

You are human, so why not celebrate being so? If you feel sad, first celebrate your humanity! It is a marvelous validation that you can experience sadness or, for that matter, all or any of the human experiences.

If you find yourself angered, go with that! Step outside yourself and see your anger, taste it, sense it.

What color is it?

What flavor is it?

How does it make you feel?

Does your heart beat faster?

Does your face get flushed?

Do your muscles tense?

What does your anger generate inside you?

All of this exploration need only take a minute or so. When you have done this examination a few times it will take far less time because anger will have become a familiar friend. You will know in advance what it is going to feel and look like.

CELEBRATE! You have just expressed your humanity. Good job. You have completely demonstrated that you are a human being.

NOW, it may not always be useful or workable to be angry at a given time.

This is the point of this book.

You now have the tools and information to choose. Sometimes it may feel wonderful or useful to go with your anger, sadness depression. So do that.

If you are driving on the highway, you may find it dangerous to get angry. Find your happiness and save the anger for later when it will not affect your safety.

If you wake up depressed, if you need to get to work, postpone the depression and get your day started and get to work.

Sometimes it is delicious to wallow in your emotion. Just make sure that you and others are safe when and where you choose to do so.

Once you have come home from work, let the people you live with know that you need five to fifteen minutes of alone time. Then go into your bedroom. Gather your tools. (ice cream, candy, teddy bear, etc.) then pull the blankets around you and do your very best job of being depressed, or sad. Go for it! Don't do a halfway job of your depression. Max your opportunity.

Cry, if that serves you.

Pout, if that serves you.

Thrash about if that serves you.

The point here is, compress your day or week of sadness or depression into no more than fifteen minutes. Less if you wish.

Anger is even easier. Get yourself into your safe space and throw a tantrum. Go crazy. Get as mad as you can. Roll on the floor and kick and scream. (make sure to inform your cohabitants in advance)

If you do not walk away emotionally spent you could have done better.

This exercise will accomplish a number of things. If you are holding onto any pent-up energy from the trigger event, this will allow you to expend that energy. You may gain some aerobic benefit from your tantrum. You will have the experience of managing your emotions so that YOU determine when you will allow them exist.

Another benefit of this practice is that you will become aware that you get to say when you are willing to experience an emotion and when you are not.

I am pumping on the chest of my inert husband. I need to keep his heart pushing fluid until the paramedics arrive. I can feel his ribs cracking under the pressure of my two hands pushing down on his chest.

They let themselves into the house and rush to take over for me. The policeman takes me into the living room.

Thus, started the closing phase of my nine-and-a-half-month long struggle to unsuccessfully cure my husband of cancer. He died under my hands, but it did not become official until later at the hospital after the doctors had made every attempt to revive him. I had spent every waking (and sleeping) moment with him, in and out of the hospital, protecting him from anything that would threaten his survival.

I was shattered as I sat, oblivious, in the waiting room of the hospital.

Grief is a wholly unsatisfactory word for the emotions that I felt.

Fast forward to a month later when I am fighting with the mortgage company since they won't allow me to take over the home loan due to the fact that we were gay and as such, in Colorado at the time, unmarried.

Everything in the World was a trigger for sadness and depression for me at the time. Denver, itself was a trigger. I found myself lapsing into bouts of crying and depression at a moment's notice.

I soon found that my grief was getting in the way of functioning as a human and even more so as a professional coach.

I started to allow 30 minute blocks of time in my schedule to wallow in my sadness each night at around eight o'clock. This gave me the freedom to make a difference for my clients and to be effective during the day.

After a month of this planned sadness process. I came to the realization that if I could control the length and hour of my sadness, then I could also control whether to give in to the sadness or not.

My eight o'clock sessions started to become shorter and less frequent. After two months, I stopped booking the sessions at all.

We, as humans, get to choose when and if we are going to indulge our emotions.

I miss my husband every minute in each day. I smile when I think of him, which is very often. I am completely grateful to him and the fact that he died so suddenly and young. Without this experience, I might never have learned how unimportant most of the trials and tribulations of life are.

And I might never have discovered that it is MY choice to live a life at the mercy of my emotions, or one that I create to be happy and joyful.

Be Happy!